Mary Seacole

Brian Williams

www.heinemann.co.uk/library
Visit our website to find out more information about **Heinemann** books.

To order:
☎ Phone 44 (0) 1865 888112
▤ Send a fax to 44 (0) 1865 314091
▢ Visit the Heinemann Bookshop at **www.heinemann.co.uk/library** to browse our catalogue and order online.

Heinemann Libraryis an imprint of Pearson Education Limited, a company incorporated in England and Wales having its registered office at Edinburgh Gate, Harlow, Essex, CM20 2JE – Registered company number: 00872828
"Heinemann" is a registered trademark of Pearson Education Limited
Text © Pearson Education Limited 2009
First published in hardback in 2009
The moral rights of the proprietor have been asserted.

Edited by Catherine Clarke and Rachel Howells
Designed by Kimberly R Miracle, Jennifer Lacki, and Betsy Wernert
Original illustrations© Pearson Education Ltd
Illustrations by Mapping Specialists
Picture research by Elizabeth Alexander
Originated by Modern Age
Printed and bound in China by Leo Paper Group

ISBN 978 0 431 04476 7 (hardback)
13 12 11 10 09
10 9 8 7 6 5 4 3 2 1

British Library Cataloguing in Publication Data
Williams, Brian, 1943-
    Mary Seacole. - (Levelled biographies)
    610.7'3'092
A full catalogue record for this book is available from the British Library.

Acknowledgements
We would like to thank the following for permission to reproduce photographs: © Alamy pp. **9** (North Wind Picture Archives), **21**, **24** (The Print Collector), **27**, **34** (Popperfoto), **41-42** (Mary Evans Picture Library), **47** (Amoret Tanner); © Corbis pp. **13**, **28** (Stapleton Collection), **22** (Kevin Schafer), **26** (Bettmann), **37** (The Gallery Collection), **45** (Historical Picture Archive); © Courtesy of Florence Nightingale Museum Trust, London pp. **30**, **43-44**; © Getty Images pp. **7** (Hulton Archive), **29** and **31** (Hulton Archive/Roger Fenton), **19** (The Bridgeman Art Library/Sir William Beechey); © Mary Evans Picture Library pp. **15** (Bruce Castle Museum), **17**, **23**; © The Bodleian Library, University of Oxford p. **46**; © The Bridgeman Art Library pp. **5**, **32**, **33** (Private Collection), **6** (DACS/J.P. Zenobel), **11** (Torre Abbey, Torquay, Devon, UK), **12** (Peabody Essex Museum, Salem, Massachusetts, USA), **14** (The Bloomsbury Workshop, London), **18**, (Christie's Images), **35** (Courtesy of the Council, National Army Museum, London); © TopFoto p. **39** (David Wimsett/UPPA. co.uk).

Cover photograph of Mary Seacole reproduced with the permission of © Getty Images (National Portrait Gallery/Albert Charles Challen).

We would like to thank Nancy Harris for her invaluable help in the preparation of this book.

Every effort has been made to contact copyright holders of any material reproduced in this book. Any omissions will be rectified in subsequent printings if notice is given to the publisher.

Disclaimer
All the Internet addresses (URLs) given in this book were valid at the time of going to press. However, due to the dynamic nature of the Internet, some addresses may have changed, or sites may have changed or ceased to exist since publication. While the author and publisher regret any inconvenience this may cause readers, no responsibility for any such changes can be accepted by either the author or the publisher.

CONTENTS

Some words are shown in bold, **like this**. You can find out what they mean by looking in the glossary.

Who was Mary Seacole?

In the **Victorian age**, few women travelled far from home, let alone across oceans and jungles. Mary Seacole did. Not many women ran businesses or saw battles. Mary Seacole did.

Most of what we know about Mary's early years comes from her own book. It was called *Wonderful Adventures of Mrs Seacole in Many Lands*, and was published in 1857. Mary was born in 1805 on the Caribbean island of Jamaica. Her full name was Mary Jane Grant. Her mother was a healer, or "doctress" as Jamaicans called her. She cared for sick people, and made her own medicines. Mary learned nursing from her mother. As a young woman, Mary visited England, where she had relatives. She got married but her husband died. She made business trips to different countries. In Panama in Central America she ran a hotel for gold-miners and travellers.

The Crimean War

In 1855, Mary Seacole went to the **Crimea**. British soldiers were fighting in the Crimean War (1853–56), and Mary wanted to help as a war nurse. When she was turned down, she went to the battlefield on her own. She provided food, clothes, and a place to rest for soldiers, and looked after the sick and wounded. This part of her life is known from letters and newspapers as well as from her book.

After the war, Mary Seacole lived in London. She died in 1881, and her name was forgotten for almost 100 years. Today, many people admire her because she was brave and did what she thought was right. She wasn't put off by danger, disease, or **racial prejudice**. She became famous in the Crimea, because she was a woman, and because she had come all the way from Jamaica to help. She was admired and respected by almost everyone, and loved by the soldiers she cared for.

This picture of Mary Seacole, in Jamaica's National Library, was painted before she went to the Crimea. Mary had enough adventures to fill several lives, but is honoured today because she risked her life to help others.

GROWING UP IN JAMAICA

Mary was born in Kingston, Jamaica, where her mother Jane ran a hotel called Blundell Hall. It was not far from the harbour. Jane was a Creole (of mixed European and African background). As well as running Blundell Hall, she also helped cure sick people, who came to her for medicines. Mary's father was a Scot. Mary says he was a soldier, and some historians think he was James Grant, an **officer** in the 60th Foot. This was an infantry **regiment** in the British Army. James Grant probably came to Jamaica with other soldiers to defend the island during Britain's wars with France. Mary was proud of her Scottish background.

This is a painting of sailing ships in the West Indies. The British navy guarded trade between Britain and its colonies.

These workers are cutting sugar cane. Cane was grown on **plantations**, large farms owned by white farmers. Until 1833, most plantation workers were slaves.

Jamaica's slaves

Jamaica was part of the **British Empire** – the overseas lands that were ruled by Britain. In the early 1800s, Britain ruled Canada, Australia, New Zealand, parts of India, and smaller places such as Jamaica and other Caribbean islands. Britain had ruled 13 North American **colonies**, until they broke away to form the United States in 1776. When Mary was born, Jamaica had approximately 300,000 people. Ninety percent of these were black. The few white settlers were mostly rich sugar cane farmers or "planters". Mary's

family was free, but most black Jamaicans were **slaves**. They, or their **ancestors**, had been brought from Africa. In 1807, the British Parliament passed a law **abolishing** the **slave trade**. After 1833 all slaves in Jamaica, and the rest of the British Empire, were free.

The slave trade

A slave is someone owned by another person, and forced to work for them. The ancient Greeks and Romans had slaves, as did the Vikings. Some were born slaves, but others were captured and made slaves. Between 1500 and 1800, it's thought that at least 12 million Africans were captured as slaves and taken to America and the Caribbean islands.

A kind "grandmother"

Mary had a younger half-brother, Edward, and a sister, Louisa. As a small child, she went to live with an elderly woman she called "my kind patroness". Mary became an extra "grandchild" in her house. The patroness may have been rich; Mary wrote that she was spoiled a little. In her book, Mary says it was only going home to her mother that stopped her growing up "idle and useless". Mary had no tolerance for people who did not get on with things, and that meant working hard.

Mary's patroness

Mary's patroness helped pay for Mary's education. A patron can be a rich person who helps someone, such as an artist or student. We do not know the name of Mary's patroness but her use of this word shows the patron was female. She may have been a rich person who was cured by Mary's mother, and in return helped with Mary's schooling. Mary loved her like an aunt or grandmother, and in her book, remembers that she "nursed [her] old indulgent patroness in her last long illness" until she died.

Home-made cures

Mary was kept busy, learning medicine from her mother. She helped with cures, and practised nursing her doll. She wrote that she loved "the rewarding glow of health" on the doll's face, when a cure worked! She tried home-made medicines on dogs and cats – and on herself. From the age of 12 she spent more time with her mother, "attending upon invalid officers or their wives" from the military camps near Kingston. Many British officers new to Jamaica developed **fevers**. A new Navy hospital was built in 1819, but in Jamaica, medicine for many was a mixture of European and African traditions. Mary's mother had plenty of patients.

Kingston was the main port of Jamaica, and a base for British navy ships and soldiers. Kingston was much livelier than the official capital, Spanish Town, and became the island's capital in 1872. Today, 700,000 people live in the city.

Up and doing

Young Mary was always busy. On the first page of her book, she writes: "All my life long I have followed the impulse which led me to be up and doing." Although historians don't know if she went to school, she learned a lot from books. She makes a joke about being a "female Ulysses" so she must have read about Ulysses, a famous traveller in Ancient Greek stories. She probably learned British and Jamaican history too. She may have studied a map of the world, to see how far away Britain was from Jamaica.

History of Jamaica

Jamaica's first people were Native Americans called Arawaks. After the Spanish conquered the island in the 1500s, the Arawaks were killed or died from diseases. African slaves were brought to work on sugar plantations, owned by white people. From 1655, Britain ruled Jamaica as a colony. Jamaica became an independent nation in 1962.

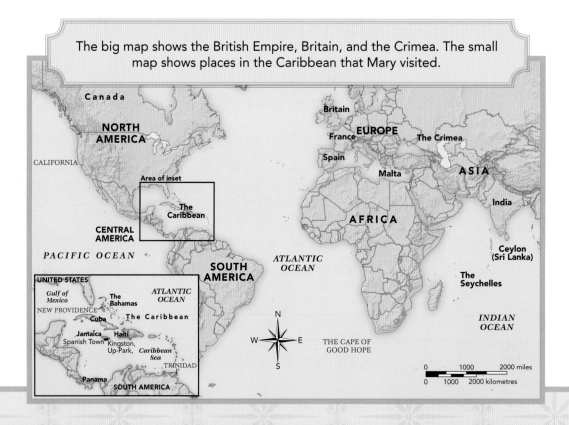

The big map shows the British Empire, Britain, and the Crimea. The small map shows places in the Caribbean that Mary visited.

British ships sailed the world, and were protected by the Royal Navy. These ships are close to home though, on the River Tyne in the north of England.

A worldwide empire

British ships sailed the world, protected by the Royal Navy, and the British Empire was growing. With Canada, Australia, New Zealand, and much of India already under British rule, Britain had gained more colonies from France during the Napoleonic Wars – such as Trinidad in the Caribbean, Malta in the Mediterranean, and the Seychelles in the Indian Ocean. Former Dutch colonies Ceylon (Sri Lanka) and the Cape of Good Hope (South Africa) had also become British.

Mary's dream

Mary's love of travel began when she was a teenager. Her home in Kingston was only a few steps from the harbour, where she watched tall-masted sailing ships coming and going. Mary dreamed of sailing to England. The chance came when she was probably about 15. Some relatives set off for England, and Mary went with them. Mary does not say who her relatives were, but they could have been members of the Henriques family, some of whom lived in London. Young Amos Henriques went from Jamaica to London to study medicine in the 1830s.

THE MOTHER COUNTRY

Mary thought of herself as British. To her, Britain was the "mother country" of the empire of which Jamaica was part. Her father had been a soldier of the **British Empire**, and she was proud of that. Soldiers and other people she met in Jamaica probably told her about life in Britain. She looked forward to seeing it for herself. A sailing ship took about six weeks to cross the Atlantic Ocean. Steamships would soon cross the ocean faster, but in the 1820s the steamship was a new invention, and Mary's first voyage to Britain was under sail.

Bristol was one of Britain's busiest ports. From Bristol, the explorer John Cabot sailed to North America in 1497. In the 18th century, Bristol grew rich on trade in sugar and **slaves**.

First sight of England

Mary's ship docked at Bristol, a port once used by slave ships. From there she rode in a **stagecoach** to London. She gazed out at the lush green fields, farms, and villages of the English countryside. How different it was from the densely forested hills of Jamaica! The journey from Bristol to London was about 190 kilometres (118 miles) and took 12 hours, with stops at inns to change horses and rest.

The Britain Mary saw

The **Industrial Revolution** brought a new age of factories, steam engines, and railways. People left farm jobs to work in factories in towns. In 1820, only 30 percent of British people lived in towns. By 1900, 80 percent did. Factories made Britain a rich and powerful country, but they brought problems too. Tiny children did dangerous factory jobs, and smoky chimneys and dirty waste made factory towns polluted.

London

When the stagecoach arrived in London, Mary was astonished. She had never seen so many buildings, or such bustling streets crowded with rich and poor people. London was growing, and Britain was changing. Soon stagecoaches would be replaced by steam trains.

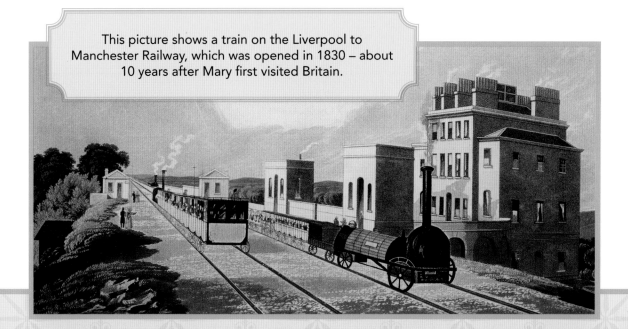

This picture shows a train on the Liverpool to Manchester Railway, which was opened in 1830 – about 10 years after Mary first visited Britain.

Black British

Black people first came to Britain with the Roman Army 2,000 years ago. In the 1800s, there were between 20,000 and 40,000 black people in Britain, out of a total population of 10.5 million. Some were important citizens. Ignatius Sancho (1729–80) owned a shop in London and for a time was an actor in the theatre. Olaudah Equiano (1745–97) campaigned against the **slave trade**. Francis Williams (lived around 1700–70) studied at Cambridge University and later ran a school in Jamaica. This painting (right) is thought to be of Francis Barber. He was the friend and servant of the writer, Dr Samuel Johnson. It was painted by Sir Joshua Reynolds in 1770.

Family connections

In London, Mary probably stayed with relatives, perhaps the Henriques family. They were in business, as traders, and had a house big enough for guests. Mary stayed about a year. She may also have met members of her father's family. Not much is known about James Grant. Army records show that his **regiment** was in Jamaica from 1802 to 1815, by which time he was a major (a middle-ranking **officer**). Mary possibly knew him until she was about 10. Nothing is known about him after that: he may have died of **fever** in Jamaica, or been sent away by the Army. He may have died before Mary came to Britain, but she could have met some of his family.

A street encounter

Mary explored London, taking in the old, interesting buildings. London was a fast-growing city; there were three times as many people living in London as there were living in Jamaica. Mary could have seen black sailors in Bristol, and other black people in London. But few British children in the 1820s would have met a black person. As Mary walked in London with another girl (perhaps her cousin), some boys made fun of the two Jamaican girls. In her book, Mary says the other girl was "very dark" and "hot-tempered", and stuck up for herself. This was Mary's first experience of **racial prejudice**.

London streets were crowded with people and traffic (horses and carts). The city was much bigger than Kingston.

A business beginning

Mary's first visit to London lasted for about one year. She was eager to return, and did so in 1823 (she was then 18). This time she stayed for two years. She visited her relatives and paid her way by selling preserves and pickles that she brought from Jamaica. It was her first business venture.

Mary would have enjoyed London's many street markets. Country folk walked in every morning with vegetables, fruit, or live geese and chickens. Dairymen sold milk, and bakers carried trays of bread. There were people selling everything you could think of, from nuts to walking sticks. Every street-seller had a cry to advertise their goods. Mary may have set up her own stall. She probably also sold medicines and gave medical advice to people, who paid for her "doctoring". Only rich people in London could afford real doctors at the time.

London's growing

From 1801, a **census** every 10 years counted the population of Britain. It shows how London grew. Nearly one million people lived in London in 1801. There were twice as many Londoners by 1841. Many poor people lived in **slums**, which were overcrowded, dirty, and unhealthy. Better-off people moved to new houses in the **suburbs**.

How London grew

Year	Population
1801	958,863
1841	1,948,417
1861	2,803,989
1881	3, 815,544

Some poor children in London were homeless. They slept on the streets, wherever they could find shelter.

A narrow escape

The voyage home to Jamaica in 1825 almost ended in disaster —there was a terrible fire on the ship. Mary asked the cook to tie her to a wooden chicken-coop, so she wouldn't drown. Luckily the flames were extinguished. This narrow escape did not stop Mary planning more trips, "with a view to gain" (making money). It's likely that she was encouraged by her time in London. She had met new people, and seen new things. She came home with lots of ideas about how to earn her own living. She was now 21. She could sell things, make medicines, and travel some more.

Marriage and miners

Mary went off on business trips to the Bahamas, Cuba, and Haiti (see map on page 10). In New Providence (the Bahamas), she sold pickles and other foods. Back in Jamaica, she nursed her patroness until the old lady died, and then returned home to her mother. There was much to do. The wives of Army **officers** often stayed at Blundell Hall, which was more comfortable than the army camp at Up Park outside Kingston. Mary was kept busy as hotel manager and nurse.

A slave rebellion

In 1831, there was a **slave** revolt in Jamaica. Twenty thousand angry slaves burned plantations and fought troops. After calm was restored, 400 slaves were hanged. In Britain, the revolt shocked people, and helped speed moves to end slavery. This happened in Jamaica (for all slaves over 21) in 1834. In her book Mary does not mention the rebellion or the freeing of the slaves.

This is a picture of Kingston as Mary knew it. The picture shows Harbour Street. British soldiers lived in camps just outside the town.

Mary gets married

On 10 November 1836, Mary Grant married Edwin Horatio Seacole. A church record of the marriage exists. Mary does not tell us much about Edwin, except that he was "very delicate" (meaning his health was poor). Historians have found out that Edwin Seacole was born in 1803. He was English, but was living in Kingston when he and Mary married. Edwin had come to Jamaica hoping to make his fortune. The Seacoles said Edwin was the **godchild** of Admiral Horatio Nelson (who was born in Norfolk). No one knows if this story is true.

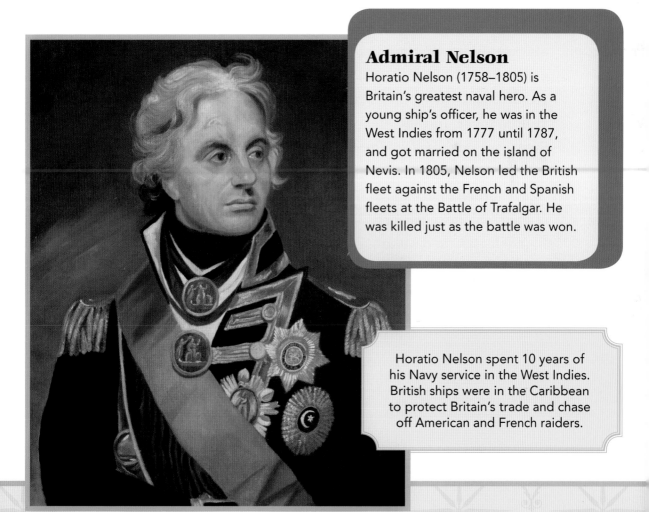

Admiral Nelson

Horatio Nelson (1758–1805) is Britain's greatest naval hero. As a young ship's officer, he was in the West Indies from 1777 until 1787, and got married on the island of Nevis. In 1805, Nelson led the British fleet against the French and Spanish fleets at the Battle of Trafalgar. He was killed just as the battle was won.

Horatio Nelson spent 10 years of his Navy service in the West Indies. British ships were in the Caribbean to protect Britain's trade and chase off American and French raiders.

Sickness and fire

The Seacoles opened a store in Black River, a busy port. Mary spent a lot of her time nursing Edwin. Doctors told her he was dying; he may have had a slowly worsening disease, such as tuberculosis. Finally, they gave up the store and moved back to Kingston. In 1843, a great fire destroyed much of the town. Mary nearly died trying to save valuables from her mother's hotel Blundell Hall, which burned down.

New Blundell Hall

In October 1844, Edwin died, leaving Mary a widow. Soon afterwards, her mother died. Mary rebuilt the hotel and called it New Blundell Hall. She treated patients from the British Army camps. Many soldiers became sick with **yellow fever**. In 1840, one in four soldiers in Kingston died from this disease. The British built a new army base at Newcastle, high in the Blue Mountains, where the climate was healthier. Mary made friends with doctors who worked at the small hospital there. They came to dinner at New Blundell Hall, and sat around her table with Army officers and their wives, who preferred the hotel to the overcrowded Army camp. Mary was becoming successful. She even had the opportunity to get married again, but she said no.

This cartoon from *Punch* magazine drew attention to the filthy state of London's river. It shows "Father Thames" introducing his "children" to the city of London (the woman in the crown). His "children" are the diseases diptheria, scrofula, and cholera. Cholera killed thousands of Londoners in the 1840s and 1850s, but it was often children who first caught these diseases.

Cholera in Jamaica

In 1850, hundreds of people began to sicken and die suddenly. Jamaica was hit by the killer-disease **cholera**. Mary worked day and night, looking after the sick. Over 30,000 people died. When the cholera was over, she decided to leave Kingston and go to Panama, where her brother Edward had opened a hotel.

Cholera

Cholera (tiny bacteria) is carried by **micro-organisms** in food or water. Dirty drinking water and bad drains are ideal breeding grounds for this infectious disease, which spreads quickly. Cholera causes severe **diarrhoea**, and victims need lots to drink. Mary knew this. She believed in fresh air, clean beds and food, and lots of water. Modern doctors agree.

Jungles and mountains made travel across Panama difficult, but the trail through Cruces saved a long sea voyage around South America.

The gold rush

In 1849, there was a **gold rush** to California, USA. To reach California from the Atlantic, travellers had either to sail around the tip of South America, or cross Panama. When she arrived in Panama, Mary thought she had never seen "a more luckless, dreary spot". With her servant Mac and her maid Mary, she went by steam train and river boat to Cruces, the town where Edward was living.

Brisk business

The hotels in Cruces were wooden huts. In Edward's hotel, Mary had to sleep under a table. She stuck to her blue dress, white bonnet, and shawl rather than wear trousers for travelling as some other women did. Business was brisk, and Mary soon opened her own hotel. She served 50 meals at a sitting, charging diners for eggs (a luxury) by the number of shells left on the plates.

These gold diggers were on their way to California. In her book, Mary says it was no use giving miners knives and forks at the dinner table, because they used their fingers to eat.

And more nursing

One traveller left disease behind in Cruces. A friend of Edward's died. When Mary saw the body, she knew it was cholera. She was kept busy nursing the sick. To learn more about the disease, she did an **autopsy** on a dead child. She returned to Jamaica in 1853, to find yellow fever again. This meant more nursing, until she went back to Panama, hoping to find gold herself.

Local delicacies

In Panama, Mary cooked salt pork, beef stew, rice, and maize (sweetcorn). She was not tempted by some local dishes: "With what pleasure could one dine off a roasted monkey?" The monkey looked like a human baby, and spooning a monkey's arm from a stew-pot made her feel ill. Parrot and squirrel were tasty, but not iguana (a kind of lizard).

A FARAWAY WAR

On her last visit to Panama, Mary met a mine manager named Thomas Day, a relative of her husband. They were soon to meet again.

Before leaving Jamaica, she had heard news of war across the ocean. France and Britain were fighting Russia, though no one seemed sure what the war was about. Turkey had gone to war with Russia because Russia had invaded Turkish territory and sunk Turkish ships in the Black Sea. Britain and France had joined in to help the Turks, because they feared Russia was becoming too strong. They chose to fight the Russians in the **Crimea**, a chunk of Russian land almost surrounded by sea, because their armies could get there in ships.

The Russian bear struggles to break loose, but the British lion is watchful. Cartoonists often drew countries as animals. This cartoon suggests that Russia started the Crimean war.

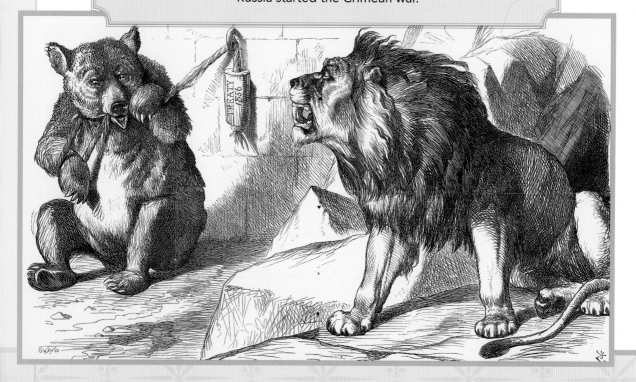

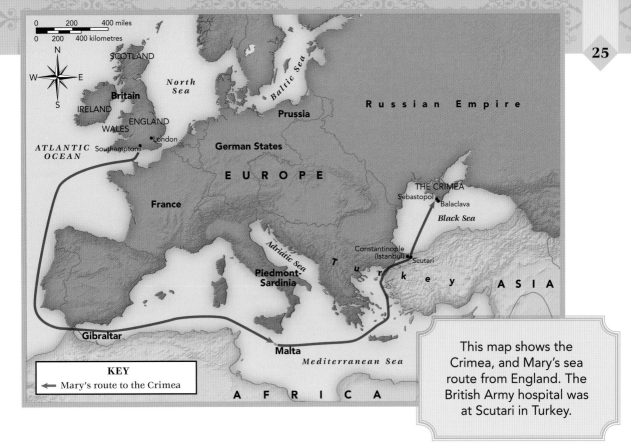

This map shows the Crimea, and Mary's sea route from England. The British Army hospital was at Scutari in Turkey.

Off to battle

Many of Mary's soldier friends in Jamaica were packing their kits, ready to sail to join the British army in battle in the Crimea. Mary had heard soldiers' stories about the horrible injuries caused by swords, rifle fire, and **cannon** balls. The Army would need nurses. Mary turned her back on Panama and its gold, and decided to head for Europe, to be a war nurse.

On a map of the world, Mary marked the Crimea with a red cross. How far away it looked! In August 1854, she sailed from Navy Bay (now Colón) in Panama. By the time her ship reached England, it was autumn. There had already been one big battle in the Crimea. Wounded men were waiting for help.

Crimean battles

In the Crimea, infantry (foot-soldiers), cavalry on horses, and artillery (big guns) often lined up facing one another. Smoke from the guns hung over the battlefield. The infantry fired rifles, which the soldier had to reload after every shot. Cavalrymen charged with lances (long spears) and curved swords called sabres.

Turned away

Mary landed at the port of Southampton on 18 October 1854. Three days later, Florence Nightingale (see box) sailed for the Crimea with 38 nurses. On 25 October, the battle of Balaclava was fought. Eleven days later there was another battle, at Inkerman. Thousands of soldiers were killed or wounded.

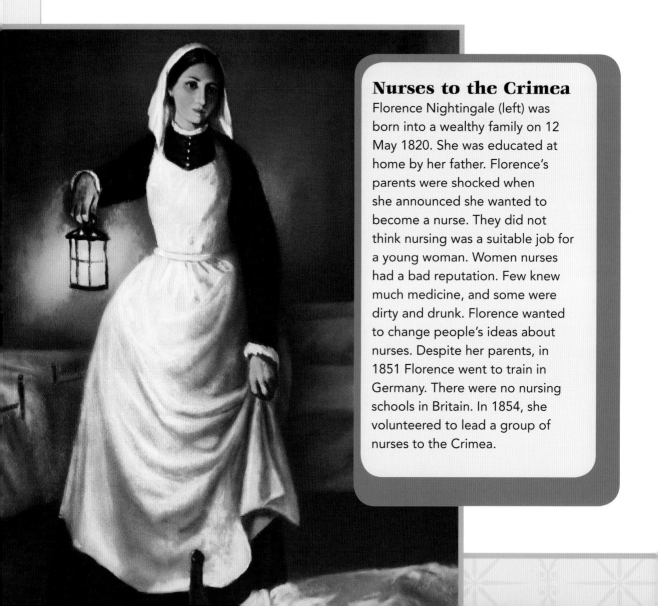

Nurses to the Crimea

Florence Nightingale (left) was born into a wealthy family on 12 May 1820. She was educated at home by her father. Florence's parents were shocked when she announced she wanted to become a nurse. They did not think nursing was a suitable job for a young woman. Women nurses had a bad reputation. Few knew much medicine, and some were dirty and drunk. Florence wanted to change people's ideas about nurses. Despite her parents, in 1851 Florence went to train in Germany. There were no nursing schools in Britain. In 1854, she volunteered to lead a group of nurses to the Crimea.

Mary went to London, to offer her help to the War Office, the government department in charge of the Army. She was turned away. She saw a friend of Florence Nightingale. The answer was still "no". In her book, Mary wrote that she saw in the woman's face that "had there been a vacancy, I should not have been chosen to fill it". Mary wondered sadly if she was rejected because of her "somewhat duskier skin" (because she was Jamaican).

Setting off on her own

Mary's nursing experience, though backed up by letters from Army friends, did not count. She was a middle-aged woman from Jamaica. No one knew her. Mary did not accept defeat. She decided to make her own way to the Crimea. She sent cards to soldier-friends already there. The cards advertised that Mrs Seacole would be arriving on the steamship *Hollander* to open a "hotel for invalids" and offer "comfortable quarters to sick and **convalescent** officers".

Steamships were the latest thing in the 1850s. This is Brunel's steamship *Great Britain*. Britain used the big ship to transport a total of 44,000 soldiers to the Crimea.

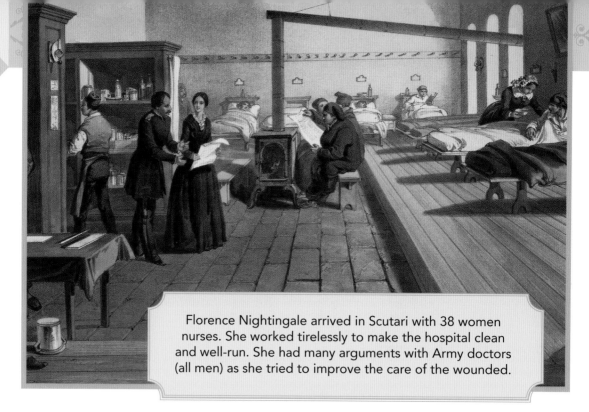

Florence Nightingale arrived in Scutari with 38 women nurses. She worked tirelessly to make the hospital clean and well-run. She had many arguments with Army doctors (all men) as she tried to improve the care of the wounded.

Seacole and Day

While in London, Mary met up again with Thomas Day. They became partners in the firm of "Seacole and Day" to run the hotel in the Crimea. Thomas sailed first. Mary bought medicines and supplies, and then she too sailed for Constantinople (now Istanbul). It was a long voyage, with stops at Gibraltar and Malta (see map on page 25), and Mary enjoyed every minute.

Mary meets Florence

From Constantinople, Mary travelled by boat to Scutari. Wounded men from the battle of Balaclava were lying in Scutari hospital. Two thousand had died in the two months before she got there. Mary met men she knew from Jamaica, soldiers of the 97th **regiment**. She also met Florence Nightingale, who offered to do "anything" for her, according to Mary, but did not ask Mary to join her team of nurses. So Mary moved on.

On to Balaclava

The cargo ship *Albatross* took Mary across the Black Sea to Balaclava. The port looked a muddle of ships, animals, wooden shacks, and people. Mary made sure her stores were unloaded, and for six weeks she camped beside them, sleeping at night on an **ammunition** ship in port. She gave hot tea to soldiers, and looked after their wounds. She and Thomas found a site on the road out of town and hired workmen to build their "British Hotel".

The charge of the Light Brigade

The battle of Balaclava was the scene of the most famous mistake in British Army history. British light cavalry – the Light Brigade – charged straight at **cannons** of the Russian Army, after the Earl of Cardigan got the orders muddled. Of 673 soldiers who charged into the "valley of death", 247 were killed or wounded.

Balaclava was muddy and full of rubbish and rats according to Mary. The harbour was jammed with up to 100 ships.

The British Hotel

Mary's hotel was made of iron sheets, and stood on a hill she named Spring Hill. It was about 6 kilometres (4 miles) outside Balaclava, on the road to the British Army camp. The Hotel had one long room, a kitchen, and store room. Mary and Thomas lived in two small outhouses. There were pig sties, cowsheds, and stables for horses. As word spread that "Mother Seacole" was in business, soldiers came crowding in.

A friendly Turkish Army commander promised to protect the store from bandits. Mary also made a good friend in Alexis Soyer. He was a French **chef**, and had been sent to the Crimea to find out how bad the soldiers' food was. Mary knew all about him (and apparently he'd also heard of her). She told him she had sold many jars of "Soyer's sauce".

This drawing of the British Hotel, called "Mrs Seacole's Hut", was made by Lady Alicia Blackwood while visiting the Crimea. She wrote a book about her adventures, and praised Mary's courage and care for the soldiers "during the time of battle, and in the time of fearful distress".

A tough winter for soldiers

In the Crimea, it was hot in summer and bitterly cold in winter. The Army did not provide extra winter clothing, and after supply ships were sunk in a storm in November 1854 many soldiers were freezing and starving. They had to buy food and drink from **civilian** traders, called sutlers. Some soldiers stole from local people or from the tents of other regiments.

British soldiers pose for a photograph. The Crimean War was the first big war in which photographers set up cameras to take pictures of soldiers and battlefields.

Mary's day

Mary was up at 5 a.m. every day and served coffee and breakfast at 7 a.m. Until midday, she tended sick and wounded soldiers. After lunch she sold goods from the store – warm clothes, hats, boots, and saddles. Her shelves were filled with tins of salmon, lobster and oysters, butter, pepper and salt, curry powder, cigars and tobacco, tea and coffee, and tooth powder. Wagons brought in fresh potatoes, carrots, turnips, and greens.

Rats, murders, and medicines

Rats swarmed everywhere. Mary's black cook, Francis, had his finger mangled while he was sleeping. A cat called Pinkie was borrowed from some soldiers to hunt the rats, but ran away. Thieves broke in to steal food, and took Mary's goats, pigs, geese, and chickens. Her washerwoman was murdered, and after that, Mary kept a gun handy.

Every day she was kept busy feeding hungry men, bandaging wounds, and treating the sick. The soldiers paid what they could, and Mary spent the money on more food, blankets, and medicines. Mary was helped by Sarah (also known as Sally) Seacole. Sally was a teenage relative of Mary's husband, and stayed with Mary until the end of the war. Then she went back to Jamaica – and disappeared from history.

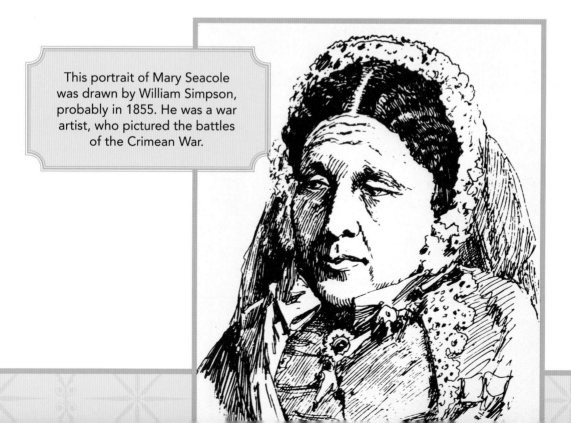

This portrait of Mary Seacole was drawn by William Simpson, probably in 1855. He was a war artist, who pictured the battles of the Crimean War.

Food at the British Hotel

The Hotel provided accommodation for sightseers, and even sold take-aways (chicken legs wrapped in paper). The meals were familiar to British soldiers: rice puddings, sausage and mash, and Welsh rarebit (a version of cheese on toast). Mary also cooked for officers' dinners. The menu for these evenings included Irish stew, goat or mutton curry, roast chicken and ham, followed by rhubarb pudding, sponge cake, and custard. Some of this food came from Britain while the rest was bought in the markets of the local towns, Kamiesch and Kadikoi. Mary sometimes added Caribbean dishes to the menu, for variety.

Alexis Soyer

Alexis Soyer, born in France in 1810, had run smart kitchens in London, and fed famine victims in Ireland, where he'd thought up a system to serve 5,000 meals of soup a day. He invented a lightweight army stove, for soldiers in the Crimea. He knew the men needed fresh food, and was impressed by Mary's cooking – 20 or more chickens a day, vegetables, and puddings. Alexis told the British Army what good work she was doing.

Alexis Soyer visits the British Hotel for a glass of wine. Mary, wearing a big hat, is standing beside him.

WONDERFUL ADVENTURES

The British Hotel was the local first-aid post, restaurant, and meeting place. Mary treated wounds, sickness, **diarrhoea**, "inflammation of the chest", and even **cholera**. She kept men cheerful when they were tired and sick, and sat with the dying. She even found beds for tourists, who came to see the war for themselves. Many soldiers wrote letters to thank her. Lord William Paulet, a senior Army **officer**, wrote in July 1856 that Mary had acted "in a most praiseworthy manner in attending wounded men, even in positions of great danger…"

William H. Russell was the first British newspaper reporter to send war news direct from the battlefield, as it was happening.

A reporter on the war

William Howard Russell (1820–1907) was a journalist who wrote about the **Crimea** for *The Times* newspaper in Britain. His reports by **telegraph** exposed the shocking shortages of food, clothing, and medicines. People were horrified when they read of the soldiers' sufferings. Russell got to know Mary, and wrote that she was "always in attendance, near the battlefield, to aid the wounded …"

Too close for comfort

Onlookers watched Crimean battles from the hilltops. Mary rode out to sell sandwiches and treat wounded men as they were carried in. At times, she went close to the fighting on horseback, with two **mules** carrying her first-aid kit. It was very dangerous when **cannon** balls smashed into the ground, as she reported, "[happened] more frequently than was agreeable".

A soldier's letter

"I certify that I was labouring under a severe attack of diarrhoea last August, and that I was restored to health through the … kindness of Mrs Seacole. I also certify that my fingers were severely jammed while working … and Mrs Seacole cured me after three doctors had fruitlessly attempted to cure them."

James Wallen, a soldier in the 5th Division Army Works Corps, wrote this letter, one of several that Mary put into her book.

These soldiers are about to fire a howitzer, a kind of cannon that fired up in the air to hit enemy soldiers in a fort.

Battlefield surgery

Clouds of smoke from the guns made it difficult to see across a Crimean battlefield. Soldiers were killed and wounded by bullets, cannon balls, sword cuts, or stabs from a bayonet (a long knife on the end of a rifle). Many wounded soldiers were left to die where they fell. Men carried back to camp often died within a day or two from infections or shock. Army surgeons **amputated** arms and legs, with no painkillers.

Into Sebastopol

In August 1855, Mary watched Russian troops driven back at the Battle of Tchernaya. She helped care for the wounded and dying from both sides. A month later, she saw British and French soldiers fighting to capture the Russian port of Sebastopol. The British lost many men during their attack on the Redan, a Russian fort. The Russians defended it fiercely with musket fire and stones dropped from the wall. The French had more success, and Sebastopol was captured. The war was over.

Crimean casualties

This table shows the numbers of soldiers, and those killed, from the five countries that fought in the Crimean War.

	Number of troops	Killed
Britain	98,000	22,000
France	309,000	95,000
Turkey	165,000	35–45,000
Piedmont-Sardinia	21,000	2,000
Russia*	325,000	134,000

*Some sources put Russian casualties higher. It's thought nearly 900,000 Russians were called up for military service (though not all in Crimean battles), and that perhaps 600,000 died, many from disease.

Mary went into the burning town, handing out drinks and food, and giving first aid. She saw many bodies, but told herself she had no time to think of the dead, when there were others "who might yet be saved". The Russian hospital was awful, with blood, bodies, and filth everywhere. She never forgot what she saw there.

In Sebastopol, victorious soldiers were celebrating. Mary collected souvenirs including a church candle and bell. A French soldier tried to arrest her as a Russian spy, until she hit him with the bell! Sightseers with sketchbooks and cameras were wandering over the battlefield. There were other women too, some nursing the wounded, some just sightseeing.

This is a painting of the battle of Sebastopol. Mary watched the fighting.

Peace in the Crimea

After the fall of Sebastopol, there were picnics, parties, and dinners at Spring Hill. The soldiers celebrated peace with horse races, cricket matches, and stage shows. Mary laughed to see bearded men struggling into her dresses, to act female parts. At Christmas, the British Hotel offered "Aunty Seacole's plum pudding", mince pies, and roast bustard (a large bird like a turkey). Mary and Thomas Day planned to enlarge the hotel, and Thomas had a scheme to hire out riding horses, because so many people were now visiting the Crimea.

Mary explored the countryside, with soldiers for company. Whenever they met Russians, her friends made out that Mary was Queen Victoria! A crowd gathered around her in one town, until Scots soldiers in kilts proved even more interesting. The Russians had never seen men wearing "skirts" before.

Homeward bound

The troops went home in the spring of 1856. It was time to pack up. Unfortunately, some of Seacole and Day's customers went home owing Mary money. The store's shelves were full, and Mary had to sell off her goods very cheaply. On 9 July there was a grand parade to say farewell to the departing soldiers.

Flies in summer

Mary was not sorry to say goodbye to the huge Crimean flies. One of her servants spent most of his day killing flies. Summer flies were a pest, biting the men at night. One **officer**, "a close relative of the Queen" (probably Count Gleichen, see page 44) complained to Mary: "they set to at night and make a supper of me".

Mary Seacole was there, and so was Alexis Soyer. Then, it was time to go. Thomas Day headed for new lands. Mary (probably with Sarah Seacole) visited "yet other lands" on the way back to England. She returned with many memories and letters of thanks, but hardly any money.

War medals
The Victoria Cross was first awarded to soldiers who had fought in the Crimea. The Queen presented the first medals in June 1857. The cross is made of bronze metal, melted down from Russian guns captured at Sebastopol. The Victoria Cross is Britain's highest award for bravery in war.

Back in England

Home again by August 1856, Mary cheered up, since "wherever I go I am sure to meet some smiling face" (old friends). She met some friends at another victory party, in London, attended by more than 2,000 soldiers. She told them that she was opening a new store in the Army town of Aldershot. The business soon failed, however, and she had to move to London, renting a room near Covent Garden market. Covent Garden was London's biggest market for fruit, vegetables, and flowers.

Times were hard. Many Crimean **veterans** were on the streets, some without jobs and some too badly injured to work at all. Mary was also in need of help. In November, a letter to *The Times* told readers about her plight: "that good old soul whose generous hospitality had warmed up many a gallant spirit" it said, was back home but penniless. Mrs Seacole had no **pension** from the government. Would friends come to her aid?

Friends in high places

General Lord Rokeby, an important friend, wrote to the newspaper to give his support (and Mary wrote back, to thank him). The humorous magazine *Punch* published a poem about Mary. The last lines asked: "What red-coat [British soldier] in all the land, but to set her on her legs again, will not lend a willing hand?"

William H. Russell visited her, and did his best to tell the world about Mary. "A more tender or skilful hand, about a wound or broken limb, could not be found among our best surgeons," he wrote in April 1857.

The power of the press

The Crimean War was the first to be covered by war reporters (like William H. Russell) and war photographers (such as Roger Fenton). Words and pictures showed people what war was really like. The power of newspapers and magazines (the press) now helped Mary Seacole, a Crimean heroine fallen on hard times. The Seacole Fund, set up to raise money for "Mother Seacole" (as many soldiers called her), was the result.

This *Punch* cartoon showed Mary handing out magazines to soldiers in hospital.

A FRIEND IN NEED

A fund-raising campaign was started for Mary. The highlight of the campaign was a series of concerts in July 1857, at the Royal Surrey Gardens in London. The show ran for 4 days, with 1,000 performers and 11 military bands. Mary was guest of honour. Newspapers reported that "the genial old lady rose from her place" to smile and wave as the audience cheered.

Mary goes into print

Mary had also written her life story. She must have worked very fast because her book was published in July 1857. She called it *Wonderful Adventures of Mrs Seacole in Many Lands*, and it became a bestseller. Money from sales of the book, and the fund-raising concerts, eased her financial worries.

Many of Mary's soldier friends came to the London concerts to show their thanks.

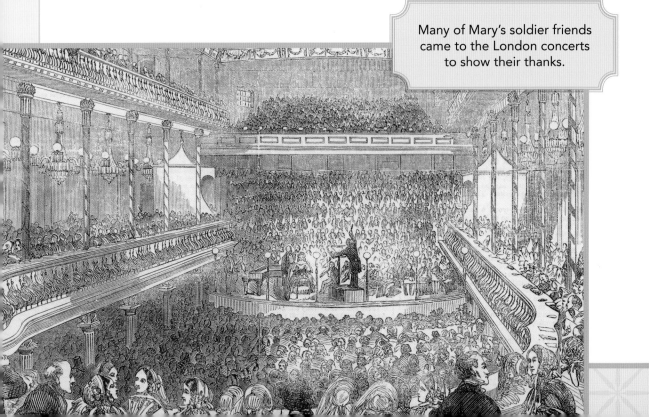

Jamaican newspapers were now following her story, and the *Daily Advertiser* (a Jamaican newspaper) reported on the London concerts, and on Mary's plans to go to India. This was her new scheme. In 1857, British soldiers were fighting Indians, in the First War of Independence or the Indian Mutiny, as it was known in Britain. Mary wanted to help, but she did not go, possibly because Queen Victoria thought Mary had done enough.

Florence Nightingale was also back in Britain. She was invited to Balmoral (the Scottish home of the Queen) and thanked in person by Queen Victoria for her work in the **Crimea**.

The Nightingale reforms

Florence Nightingale was shy (unlike Mary) and did not like publicity, but she used her fame to push for **reforms** in Army medicine and nurse-training. She became ill and collapsed in 1857, and never again appeared in public. In 1860, the Nightingale School for Nurses opened at St Thomas's Hospital in London. Mary Seacole and Florence Nightingale were both great women, in different ways. Florence won a worldwide reputation in her lifetime, as the founder of modern nursing. She died in 1910.

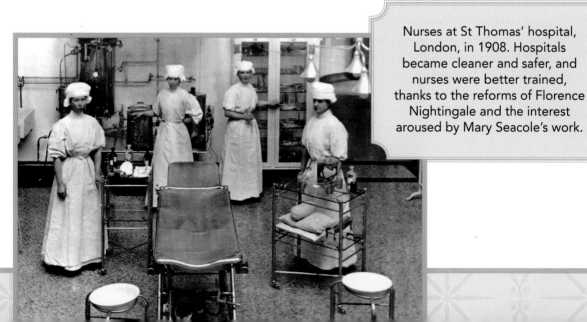

Nurses at St Thomas' hospital, London, in 1908. Hospitals became cleaner and safer, and nurses were better trained, thanks to the reforms of Florence Nightingale and the interest aroused by Mary Seacole's work.

Mary's later years

Around 1858–60, Mary bought a home in Jamaica. She may have wanted to escape the damp, foggy London winters. A second fund to help her, in 1867, was supported by Queen Victoria's son, the Prince of Wales. Mary gave the Princess of Wales massages for her rheumatism.

One last "no"

In 1870, France and Prussia went to war. *The Times* newspaper asked for volunteers to give first aid to the wounded. Although she was 65 years old, Mary wanted to go, but she was not invited.

One possible reason was a letter that Florence Nightingale sent to her brother-in-law, Sir Harry Verney, a Member of Parliament helping to recruit first-aid volunteers. In August 1870, Florence wrote that in the Crimea Mary "was very kind to the men ... and did some good", but there were rumours of "drunkenness and improper conduct". She had tried to keep Mrs Seacole away from her nurses.

The Victoria connection

Victoria was Britain's queen from 1837 until 1901. Her eldest son was the Prince of Wales, later King Edward VII, who gave money to the Mary Seacole fund. One of the Queen's many nephews was Prince Viktor, Count Gleichen (1833–91). He was in the Royal Navy during the Crimean War. He became a sculptor and made the **bust** of Mary.

In 1872, this bust of Mary sculpted by Count Gleichen was exhibited at the Royal Academy in London.

Why did Florence take this view of Mary? Perhaps because she was very prim and proper, while Mary liked to joke (and share a glass of wine) with the soldiers she called "my sons". They were very different people.

Mary dies

From the 1870s Mary lived quietly in London. She died at her Paddington home on 14 May 1881. She was 76. In her **will**, she left money and property (she now owned two houses in Kingston) to her family and friends. Thomas Day got £19, and 19 shillings; Lord Rokeby got £50; a home for the **orphans** of soldiers got £100.

Mary lived at Portman Square in London in the 1870s.

MARY'S LEGACY

In 1903, Mary was mentioned in a book of *Noble Deeds of the World's Heroines*, but by then most people had forgotten her. In 1938, someone wrote to the *Sunday Times* newspaper, asking about a picture of "Mrs Seacole". Did anyone know who she was?

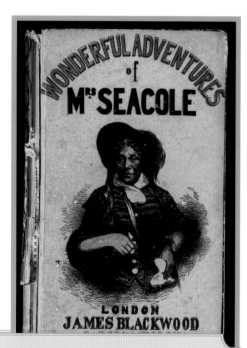

The front cover of Mary's book, published in 1857, shows her wearing a floppy hat, and an Army-style dress with brass buttons. She has a bag slung around her neck.

Mary is rediscovered

Interest in Mary reawakened 100 years after the **Crimean** War. People read her book, and in 1954, the headquarters of the Nurses Association in Jamaica was named after her. In the 1970s, her grave in London was restored. By the 1990s she was well-known again, and people were looking at her life with new interest. They were particularly interested in her experiences as a woman, making her own way in the world, as a traveller and in business. In 2004, she was named the greatest "black Briton" in history.

Seacole and Nightingale

People often compare Mary Seacole and Florence Nightingale. Both were brave, determined people. Their backgrounds, and nursing methods, were very different. Florence is famous for her **reforms** (changes) to nursing. Mary is famous for being "Mother Seacole", the soldiers' friend.

A remarkable life

What makes Mary Seacole remarkable, and a good role model, is the way that she lived. She was independent, caring, and good-humoured. She helped others, and was unafraid of dangers, disease, and **racial prejudice**.

The only known photograph of Mary was taken around 1873. She was then 68. It was a small "visiting card" portrait, taken in a photographer's studio, and she chose to be pictured mixing some kind of medicine.

Black heroine

Mary thought of herself as British, too pale-skinned to be "black Jamaican". "I am only a little brown" she writes in her book. She was proud to be half-Scottish. She met people who treated her unkindly because of her skin colour, but no soldier in the Crimea minded who she was or where she came from.

TIMELINES

Mary Seacole's life

1805	Mary is born in Jamaica.
1817	Mary helps her mother treat soldiers from Up-Park and Newcastle camps in Jamaica.
1820s	Mary visits Britain twice. She also travels to the Bahamas, Haiti, and Cuba.
1831	**Slave** uprising occurs in Jamaica.
1836	Mary marries Edwin Horatio Seacole.
1843	Fire in Kingston burns down Blundell Hall, the hotel owned by Mary's mother.
1844	Edwin dies. Mary's mother dies.
1850	Mary helps nurse **cholera** victims in Jamaica.
1852	Mary visits her brother, Edward, in Panama and opens a hotel in Cruces.
1853	Back in Jamaica, she helps fight **yellow fever**. In Panama, she tries her hand at gold-prospecting. She meets Thomas Day.
OCTOBER 1854	Mary arrives in England. She wants to work as a nurse in the **Crimea**, but is rejected. She goes into partnership with Thomas Day.
FEBRUARY 1855	Mary travels to the Crimea. She meets Florence Nightingale. She crosses the Black Sea to Balaclava. She and Thomas open the "British Hotel".

April 1855 Mary looks after the sick and wounded during the attack on Sebastopol. She meets French chef Alexis Soyer.

August/September

1855 Battle of Tchernaya. Mary treats French, Sardinian, and Russian soldiers. French and British troops occupy the ruins of Sebastopol. Mary enters the ruined town.

March 1856 Crimean War ends. Mary returns to England. In October, the firm of Seacole and Day is declared bankrupt (has no money).

1857 The Seacole Fund is set up. Friends arrange concerts to raise money for Mary. Her book *Wonderful Adventures of Mrs Seacole in Many Lands* is published. Mary tells friends she wants to go to India.

1858 Mary's friend Alexis Soyer dies.

1859 Mary buys a home in Jamaica.

1867 A second fund-raising committee is set up to help Mary.

1870 Mary wants to go to France, to nurse soldiers in the Franco-Prussian War.

1872 A **bust** of Mary is displayed at the Royal Academy in London.

1881 Mary Seacole dies after a stroke. She is buried in Kensal Green Cemetery in London, not far from the grave of her old friend Alexis Soyer.

World timeline

1805   Birth of Mary Jane Grant (Mary Seacole). Battle of Trafalgar.

1815   Battle of Waterloo. End of the Napoleonic Wars.

1830   The world's first steam passenger railway is opened in Britain.

1833   All slaves in the **British Empire** are freed by law.

1838   Queen Victoria is crowned in Westminster Abbey, London.

1847   The 10-hour Act limits the working day of women and children in Britain.

1848   The first public health laws in Britain.

1851   The Great Exhibition, at the Crystal Palace in Hyde Park, London. It shows off the inventions of the **Victorian age**.

1853   Turkey declares war on Russia; the Crimean War begins.

1854   60,000 soldiers from Britain and France land in the Crimea; battles of the Alma, Inkerman, and Balaclava.

1855   Capture of Sebastopol by British and French troops.

1856   Crimean War ends.

1857   Revolution or mutiny in India, as Indian soldiers rebel against British rule.

1860 Florence Nightingale starts Britain's first training school for nurses.

1861 Death of Queen Victoria's husband Prince Albert. The American Civil War begins.

1865 End of the American Civil War. Slavery is **abolished** in the United States.

1865 Morant Bay Rebellion in Jamaica. British governor Edward Eyre is blamed for acting harshly.

1876 Alexander Graham Bell invents the telephone.

1879 Thomas Edison switches on the first electric light bulb.

1881 Death of Mary Seacole in London.

1881 Flogging (beating) is ended as a punishment in the British Army.

1901 Death of Queen Victoria.

1910 Death of Florence Nightingale.

1954 Jamaican nurses rename their headquarters building "Mary Seacole House".

1973 Mary's grave in London is restored.

1990 Mary is awarded Jamaica's Order of Merit.

2005 Jamaica issues commemorative stamps in honour of the 200th anniversary of Mary Seacole's birth.

Glossary

abolish to abolish a custom or practice is to stop it by passing a law against it, for example the abolition of the slave trade

ammunition rifle bullets, cannon balls, and gunpowder

amputate to cut off, by a doctor as part of medical treatment

ancestor grandparent or other distant relative

autopsy study of the inside of a dead body, after it has been cut open with a knife

British Empire countries ruled by Britain or linked to it

bust sculpture usually in stone or bronze that shows the head and shoulders of a person

cannon big gun, pulled by horses, that fired solid metal balls or exploding shells

census count and survey of all the people in a country. Britain's 10-year census began in 1801.

chef cook in a hotel or restaurant

cholera dangerous disease causing sickness and diarrhoea

civilian person who is not in the armed forces

colony territory ruled or settled by people from another country

convalescent recovering from illness or injury

Crimea area of land, almost surrounded by the Black Sea, now part of Ukraine

diarrhoea sickness that makes a person have too many bowel movements (going to the toilet)

fever illness producing a high temperature and sweating; sometimes leading to death

general officer of high military rank

godchild someone with godparents – adults not their birth-parents – who agree to help raise him or her in the Christian religion

gold rush discovery of gold. There were famous gold rushes to California in 1848, and to Australia in 1851.

Industrial revolution period in the late 18th and 19th centuries, also known as the factory or steam age

micro-organism tiny bacteria

mule animal that is a cross between a horse and donkey

officer someone in the army who gives orders, holding the rank of lieutenant or above

orphan child whose natural parents (mother and father) are dead

pension money paid to a person retired from work

plantation large farm, where one crop, such as sugar, is grown

racial prejudice unfair treatment of other people because of their race or skin colour

reforms changes in laws, to make things better for people

regiment unit or large body of men in an army, with its own name or number, led by a colonel

slave servant or worker who is not free, but owned by another person

slave trade buying and selling of people as slaves

slum district with poor, overcrowded housing

stagecoach horse-drawn vehicle that carried passengers

suburb residential area some distance from the centre of a town

telegraph system for sending messages in code electrically through wires

veteran ex-member of the armed forces

Victorian age period of history covering the reign of Queen Victoria, 1837–1901

will last wishes of a dying person, written down as a legal document

yellow fever tropical disease spread by mosquito bites

Want to know more?

Books

Mary Seacole: A Story from the Crimean War, Sam Godwin (Hodder
   Wayland, 2001)

Tell Me About: Mary Seacole, John Malam (Evans Brothers, 2004)

The Life and World of Mary Seacole, Brian Williams
   (Heinemann Library, 2003)

Wonderful Adventures of Mrs Seacole in Many Lands, Mary Seacole
   (Penguin Classics, 2005)

Websites

www.bbc.co.uk/history/historic_figures/seacole_mary.shtml
A description of the life of Mary Seacole.

www.maryseacole.com
The website of the Mary Seacole Centre has details of places and
institutions named after her.

www.nlj.org.jm/biographies.htm
Mary Seacole's life is described on the National Library of
Jamaica's website.

Places to visit

Imperial War Museum
Lambeth Road • London SE1 6HZ • Tel: 020 7416 5320/ 5321
www.iwm.org.uk

National Army Museum
Lambeth Road • London SE1 6HZ • Tel: 020 7416 5320/ 5321
www.national-army-museum.ac.uk

Royal Armouries Museum
Armouries Drive • Leeds • West Yorkshire LS10 1LT • Tel: 0113 220 1916
www.royalarmouries.org
These three museums of military history and technology are good places
to visit to find out more about army life in Mary Seacole's day, and to
learn about the battles of the Crimean War.

Florence Nightingale Museum
St Thomas's Hospital • 2 Lambeth Palace Road • London SE1 7EW
Tel: 020 7620 0374 • Email: info@florence-nightingale.com
This museum is in the hospital where Florence Nightingale started
Britain's first school for nurses, and it also features the work of Mary
Seacole in the Crimea.

INDEX